The Page Power: Success Made Simple

Stacie K. Cottrell

Copyright

All rights reserved. No part of this publication may be reproduce, distributed or transmitted in any form or by any means including Photocopying, recording or any other electronic or mechanical methods without the prior written permission of the publisher. Except in the case of brief quotations embodied in critical reviews and certain other noncommercial uses permitted by copyright law.
Copyright © Stacie K. Cottrell / 2024

INTRODUCTION
WHY DO I NEED A MARKETING PLAN ANYWAY?
Chapter 1
Choose The Ideal Customers for your Business
Chapter 2
Develop your message
Why message development matters
Chapter 3
Reaching out to potential customers through advertisement
Chapter 4
Get Catchy Lead
Chapter 5
Supporting Leads
Chapter 6
Sales Conversion
Chapter 7
Increasing customer lifetime value
Chapter 8
Organizing and animating reference
This is deep.
Conclusion

INTRODUCTION

Organizations of all sizes share one thing practically speaking: They all started as private companies. Beginning little is the corner for those simply making headway. Find out about how to make that first recruit, manage everything authoritative, and put yourself in a good position.

A showcasing plan is an outline for sending off new items, grasping the complexities of your market, developing your crowd, and elevating your organization to clients who need what you're selling.

With a very much planned showcasing plan, you can plan more viable advancements and significant missions, arrive at your clients with designated promotion, and track your business accomplishment with examination. Without one, you should toss your showcasing spending plan down a well and stay optimistic.

On the off chance that you've been entrusted with making a promoting plan for your organization, there are a fundamental components to remember. However every showcasing plan will mirror the particular business and industry it's been made for, most offer a couple of normal highlights and can be reduced to only a couple of basic targets.

A showcasing plan is an outline for sending off new items, figuring out the complexities of your market, developing your crowd, and elevating your organization to clients who need what you're selling.

With a very much planned showcasing plan, you can plan more viable advancements and effective missions, arrive at your clients with designated promoting, and track your business accomplishment with examination. Without one, you should toss your showcasing spending plan down a well and hold out for divine intervention.

To comprehend the reason why a showcasing plan is significant, simply consider what might occur without one. Your publicizing financial plan would be spent on mystery about where your potential clients can be found and what they're searching for. You'd have no clue about which of your missions added to expanded marketing projections. Furthermore, you'd have no baselines from which to fabricate more powerful missions later on.

In a world saturated with information overload and marketing noise, simplicity reigns supreme as the ultimate disruptor. Welcome to the realm of "The page power : Success Made Simple," where we embark on a journey to unlock the transformative power of concise communication and streamlined strategies.

Imagine flipping through a single page—a canvas of clarity and precision—where all the complexities of marketing dissolve into a straightforward roadmap to success. This is not just a dream; it's the reality awaiting you within the pages of this revolutionary book.

Gone are the days of drowning in endless data and convoluted plans. Instead, we embrace the elegance of simplicity, distilling the essence of effective marketing into a concise masterpiece that resonates with your audience on a profound level.

But simplicity doesn't mean sacrificing substance. In fact, it's quite the opposite. Each word, each element carefully chosen on your 1-page marketing canvas packs a punch, delivering a message that cuts through the noise and leaves a lasting impression.

Within these pages, you'll discover the secrets to crafting compelling narratives, defining your unique value proposition, and connecting authentically with your target market. Through real-world examples, actionable insights, and practical strategies, we'll show you how to harness the power of simplicity to drive meaningful results and propel your brand to new heights of success.

Whether you're a seasoned marketing guru looking for fresh inspiration or an entrepreneur seeking a straightforward approach to building your brand, "The page power : Success Made Simple" is your guidebook to unlocking untold opportunities in a cluttered world. Join us as we demystify the complexities of marketing and prove that success doesn't have to be complicated—it can be as simple as a single page. Get ready to unleash the magic and make success simple.

WHY DO I NEED A MARKETING PLAN ANYWAY?

As fellow business proprietors, we understand the value of time, as there's always an abundance of tasks and limited time to accomplish them. Thus, what exactly is the necessity for a marketing strategy?

It's common for humans to procrastinate tasks that are unfamiliar or not deemed urgent. Allocating time to craft a marketing plan often falls into this category. People may say, 'It would be nice to do, but we're short on time,' 'We're doing fine without one,' 'We're unsure where to begin,' or dismiss marketing as mere fluff.

We encourage reconsideration because without a plan, it's challenging to navigate your business's direction.

Here are reasons why dedicating time to develop a marketing plan is crucial. Although it demands research, time, and commitment, it's a valuable process that significantly contributes to business success.

- A marketing plan prompts consideration of the broader perspective amidst the daily flurry of tasks. Drafting this plan prompts reflection on past experiences and future aspirations. It aids in identifying external opportunities and threats, internal strengths to leverage, and weaknesses to address. By documenting ideas, rather than keeping them confined to thoughts, you enhance the likelihood of implementing great concepts.

- Moreover, it ensures alignment between marketing endeavors and overarching business strategy. Amidst the hustle, maintaining focus on business goals can be challenging. A well-crafted marketing plan delineates clear objectives, tasks, responsible parties, and timelines, thereby averting distractions and preserving focus.

- Furthermore, it facilitates the discovery of your business's unique attributes. Brand development is integral to business growth. Through meticulous planning, you discern your target market, comprehend their needs, assess competitors' strengths and weaknesses, and strategically position your brand.

- Additionally, it empowers you to take charge of your business operations. Setting specific, measurable goals, establishing timelines, allocating resources, and delineating budgets streamline day-to-day activities. The upfront effort yields long-term benefits, serving as a reference point and guide for subsequent years' objectives and strategies.

- Lastly, it enables the assessment of investment value. A well-structured marketing plan delineates expenditure allocation, aiding in expenditure management, cash flow monitoring, and assessing marketing efficacy. It evolves into a dynamic tool for gauging sales performance, customer retention, product evolution, and sales initiatives.

Chapter 1

Choose The Ideal Customers for your Business

Picking the appropriate clients for your business is basic for development. Zeroing in on getting more clients for your association without first figuring out who the ideal clients are can be impeding to its prosperity. Assuming you target everybody in your client chase, you won't reach or address the issues of anybody. Notwithstanding, separating the right customers, not to mention screening them for practicality, is a consistent test. This book will acquaint you with the standards of tracking down the best customers for your business.

Most associations serve more than one kind of client. Your indispensable client, otherwise called a middle or basic client, is the one you'll address first with your future drives in general. This incorporates things like creating business methodology through promoting and item progression.

Despite the fact that they could utilize your items or administrations, helper clients are normally less dynamic or useful than key clients.

The best situation to Pick the Right visitors for Your Business

There are a large number of approaches to finding and picking the trendy visitors for your business. The most notable and significant ways for risking new visitors are represented below;

- **Begin by distinguishing the issue your item or administration tackles.**
  Try not to ponder the elements or advantages. Check it out according to a client viewpoint. What trouble spot could somebody must have to need what you're advertising? For instance, in the event that you run a shipping organization, you could begin with the possibility that the client has products that should be moved. That is a beginning, however you can trim it down more.

- **Consider What Kind of Clients You Don't Need**

Numerous entrepreneurs don't consider who they would rather not serve while tracking down clients for their business, yet it's similarly essentially as significant as characterizing who you would like to target. The standards for client determination will change from one business to the next. Consider who has the issue you are solving. There may be various client types here, so make a rundown.

Then, recognize the socioeconomics and attributes for every client type you've recorded. Make note of things like strength, years in business, and area. It's smart to write down what they esteem also. For instance, they might put orders in light of cost, saw esteem, nature of administration or item, or master information. Consider who you can serve best. You might wind up checking client types off the client procurement list completely at this step. You're likewise prone to find that a portion of those you've recorded benefit from your items or administrations more than others. They'll be your competitors for essential clients.

Furthermore, You might have the option to recognize a portion of these clients in light of your own insight, yet remember to investigate your information here as well.

- **Guarantee the Clients You Pick Are Productive**

You've most likely found that you can help many kinds of clients, however it's not generally in your business' wellbeing to do as such. They'll have to carry worth to your association to be viewed as essential clients.

- **Lifetime Worth**

The lifetime worth of a not entirely settled client by duplicating their typical request esteem, request recurrence, and life expectancy. The more prominent the lifetime esteem, the more assets you can commit to drawing in and holding the client type.

- **Payment Terms**

Installment terms, or the states of your request/buy understanding, incorporate things like how long a client needs to pay their receipt, in the event that cash is expected forthright, how huge of a request a client can put, late expenses, and some other rules you lay out. You'll need to check out at it in two unique ways.

In the first place, consider installment terms on a wide scale for every client type you're thinking about serving, both as far as industry guidelines and what sorts of terms a regular client inside that specialty would require. Then, at that point, vet individual planned clients by similar standards. On the off chance that they need longer terms or more adaptable installment choices than your organization can give, you'll either have to eliminate them from your possibility of rundown or track down a substitute method for addressing their requirements, for example, _receipt figuring_.

- **Financial soundness**

An iimportant part of finding the right clients for your business is assessing the credit chronicles of likely clients to decide whether they are installment gambles or not. At the point when you receive clients for work or merchandise after they've been conveyed, you're expanding credit. It means a lot to look into the financial soundness of individual clients prior to consenting to any sort of broadened installment terms hence

For representation, on the off chance that you run a very good quality brand, you don't have any desire to draw in economical visitors or the people who come to you asking at youuur ongoing Clients

In the event that your business is now in activity, your ongoing client base will probably point you in the correct course. Keep in mind, in any case, that you can't simply check out all your client information in one area. All things being equal, you need to pick the information apart. Let's say your CRM information shows that

60% of your clients are male, and their typical age is 45. It's not difficult to think this is your essential client.

Yet, maybe assuming you drill down the information, you'll discover that these clients just submit a request with you once and afterward leave. Perhaps your 30-year-old female clients submit rehash requests and are, in this manner, they're the you need to work with more.

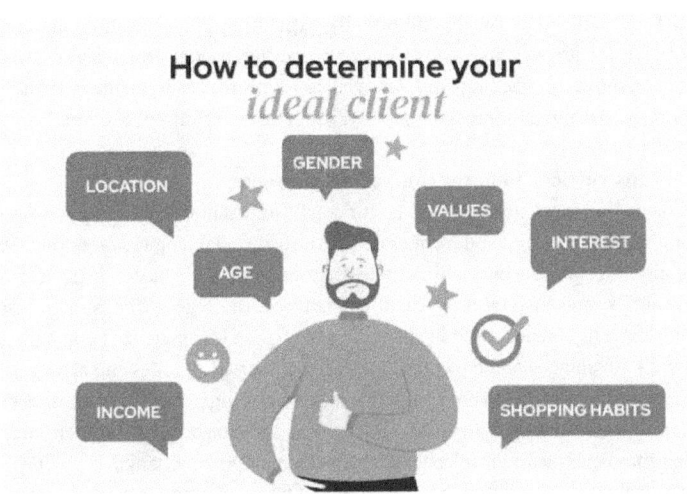

Chapter 2

Develop your message

Why message development matters

Message development isn't just about making engaging mottos or titles, yet additionally about associating your correspondence with your methodology, character, and values. It can assist with characterizing your novel offer and separate you from contenders, while additionally explaining goals and how to accomplish them. Moreover, message improvement can draw in your crowd and rouse them to make a move or backing you, as well as reinforce your image personality and notoriety. Also, it can forestall disarray, irregularity, or misconception.

Instructions to foster compelling messages

Message advancement is a continuous interaction that requires research, examination, testing, and refinement. To foster viable messages, you ought to initially recognize your main interest group and their necessities, inclinations, difficulties, and inspirations. Then, characterize the reason and wanted results for every correspondence circumstance. Conceptualize key messages that address your crowd's advantages and concerns, and feature your advantages and arrangements.

Subsequently, sort out your messages into an intelligent and cognizant design, *for example, the message pyramid or the message map model*. Furthermore, create your messages utilizing clear, compact and convincing language while keeping away from sensitive language or specialized terms. At long last, test your messages with your crowd to get input and refine them in light of the criticism.

At the point when we discuss brands, logos and pictures are the principal things that ring a bell. In any case, something significant that characterizes a brand and separates it from its rivals is its " Center **MESSAGE**". A center message is significant at all degrees of business as well with regards to all sizes of business. Distinguishing your center message has both short and long haul benefits for your business.It assists you with showcasing your image better and singles you out from your rivals.

Karen Kang, a brand planner says that, to prevail with regards to marketing, you should recognize the absolute most significant thing to be known for and reliably brand around it. Your center message is the bedrock of your business. When you can put the nail on what truly reverberates, feel free to make your center message around it. The most genuine method for carrying on with work, is to maintain your business in accordance with your center convictions, values and reason.

Here are ways you can make an enrapturing message for your business:

Recognize Your Crowd: Your image technique relies to a great extent upon your crowd. It is in recognizing your crowd that you can make your message to straightforwardly address them. You ought to make purchaser personas that distinguish your optimal clients. Then, make your substance to proactively show to your clients that your image can take care of their concerns. Load your content with information that speaks directly to your customers' needs.

- Be Particular with Your Phrasing: Making a message isn't generally about sounding wise however, cleverly conveying your image's capacities such that makes clients make a move. Keep away from the utilization of large or uncertain words, don't go off on bunny trails, giving data that are superfluous. Convey your message compactly with the utilization of solid and brief words.
- Distinguish Your One of a kind Selling Point: Consider what interestingly separates your image from your rivals, then use it to give an unmistakable very much imparted message to your main interest group. Fabricate your message around it, and watch sell your image easily. Likewise, let your message mirror your business' central goal and worth guarantee to your clients. This will empower you to adjust your message to your organization's objectives. Convey a mission statement, and let your client know where you stand and a big motivator for you.
- I know this sounds bizarre however, research your rivals' information. Knowing your rivals' informing, is basic to your business achievement. You want to foster a covert operative strategy to keep you in the loop of what message your rival is selling. Gain from their mix-ups, archive what works, and really make separation in the commercial center. Feel free to survey your rivals ' sites and social media now and again. You can likewise set google marks for contests aware of knowing when they are in the information.
- Make a Profound Association With Your Message: When your message makes and close to home association you are winning. Profound bond is basic. Business Wire Study (2018), puts it that, Close to home association is the most prescient power behind brand buying choices and long haul steadfastness of shoppers. Your message should consider snatch. The objective ought to be a rapidly cause to notice your image/brand and that takes an inventiveness and assurance

to track down a couple of certifiable words that stop customers in their tracks.

Follow the Five Cs for Successful Messaging

- Clear: Easy to understand and remember no matter the audience.
- Concise: Direct and to the point without unnecessary insertions that may distract audiences from the main points.
- Credible: Believable in that the messages are backed by proof points and incorporate supporting details to strengthen the key points.
- Compelling: Catches your audiences' attention and inspires them to take applicable action.
- Consistent: Repeatable and flexible enough to be incorporated into varying communications channels again and again

To be clear, message creation is not the same as a script. There is no replacement for thoughtful, strategic core messages that are customized to your individual audiences. You can have the best design or visual effects, perfect timing, and spot-on delivery, but none of that matters if your messages aren't created in a way that your audiences can hear and digest them.

For example, sometimes we share too much information, or information that's hard to digest, and therefore causes confusion and sometimes, even anxiety. Once you have messages that meet an audience's mindset, find opportunities to weave your messages into different communication mediums.

So now you know the Five Cs, but what next? Follow these steps for developing your core messages and you'll provide yourself and your audience with the foundational building blocks for successful communications.

Chapter 3

Reaching out to potential customers through advertisement

Connecting with potential clients can be a test, particularly in the present serious market. With the right methodology and technique, in any case, you can ensure that your message gets heard by individuals who make the biggest difference. Whether it's through online entertainment, email crusades, or customary promoting techniques like print or TV advertisements, there are different ways of contacting possible clients. Here are the absolute best methodologies for associating with your main interest group and getting them intrigued by what you bring to the table.

1. . **Web Advancement**

To ensure potential clients can find your business on the web, web advancement is a significant stage. Putting resources into a site that is very much planned, enhanced for web crawlers, and simple to explore will assist you with contacting more individuals. You ought to likewise make accounts on famous web-based entertainment destinations like Facebook, Twitter, Instagram, or LinkedIn so you can assemble associations with possible clients. Moreover, by employing web improvement administrations, you can have custom web architectures with every one of the elements and capabilities your business needs. It's likewise essential to have a blog or content showcasing procedure set up to keep potential clients locked in

2. **Paid Publicizing**

Paid publicizing is one more viable method for arriving at likely clients. Paid promoting permits you to target explicit crowds so your message will be seen by those probably going to answer decidedly. It additionally empowers you to track and quantify the outcome of your mission, making it simpler to advance and refine it for expanded execution over the long haul. With different stages accessible like Google Advertisements, Facebook Promotions, LinkedIn Promotions, and that's only the tip of the iceberg, there are a lot of choices for making efforts that can be custom-made to meet any financial plan or objective.

3. **Email Showcasing**

Email showcasing is an incredible method for arriving at likely clients and keep them informed about your items or administrations. You can make modified messages with designated content for explicit crowds, permitting you to create a message that talks straightforwardly to their inclinations and necessities. Moreover, email crusades are profoundly identifiable, so you can without much of a stretch measure the outcome of your endeavors and change likewise. Assuming done well, email showcasing can be a compelling device in laying out associations with expected clients and aiding drive changes. While it can require a huge speculation of time and exertion, the potential prizes make it an important device for any business hoping to develop.

4. **Organizing Occasions**

Organizing occasions are perfect for meeting likely clients. Besides the fact that you get to meet a many individuals immediately, however you likewise have the chance to give your brief presentation and trade business cards. Remember that systems administration occasions are tied in with framing connections, not tied in with pitching items or administrations. You need to be viewed as a supportive asset, so center around building entrust with others instead of essentially attempting to make fast deals. Organizing occasions frequently incorporate specialists from related ventures who can give important knowledge into your objective market, so consider them a fantastic wellspring of data gathering too! Furthermore, going to industry occasions can assist with building memorability and lay out validity inside the local area which can eventually prompt more deals down the line.

5. Informal exchange

Informal exchange can be the best method for connecting with likely clients. It's been said that one fulfilled client is worth in excess of ten obtained through different strategies. Individuals will quite often believe proposals from individuals they know, so it's essential to get your ongoing clients discussing you and your business. Empowering them to impart their encounters to others will assist with getting the message out about your image and make a compounding phenomenon. This could include offering limits or awards for references or simply requesting that clients share their encounters via online entertainment.

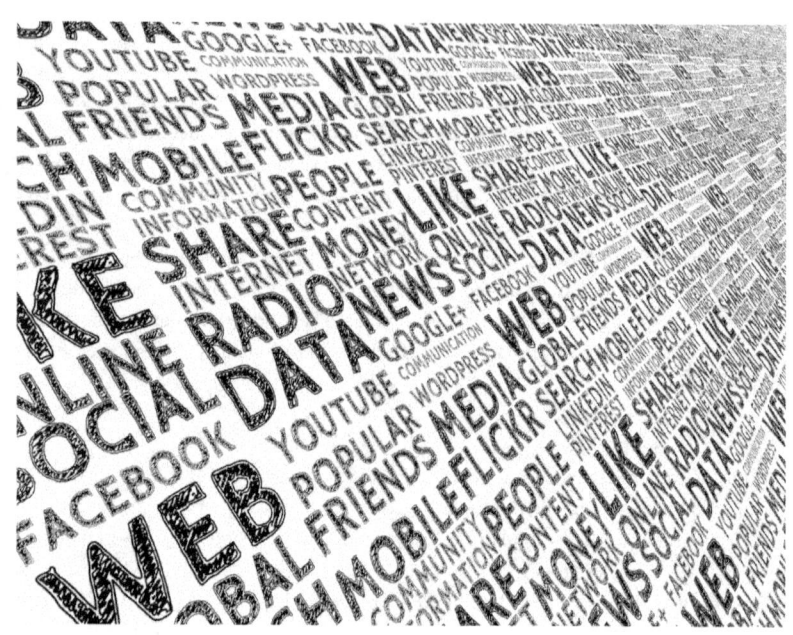

Chapter 4

Get Catchy Lead

In my profession of business, I am yet to meet an individual who has conceded that leads are NOT significant for their business. Having said that, I am yet to meet an individual who might characterize precisely for what reason is is sgnificant. *It resembles drinking water*. We as a whole vibe the need to figure out the significance however it takes cognizant endeavors to consume it and remain solid!

So here are the primary motivations behind why they are significant and how to put forth cognizant attempts to produce leads for a solid business.

    1. **Focusing on wanted clients**: More regularly, individuals wind up serving individuals who are giving them business as opposed to requesting business from explicit individuals. To repeat, it's clients choosing the value of the items/administration as opposed to an entrepreneur taking care of a particular issue and requesting cash for something very similar. Thus, pay special attention to a particular crowd to take care of the issue.

    2. **Get perceivability:** Chasing after great leads additionally supports brand perceivability which likewise helps for brand mindfulness.

    3. **Leads and benefits**: Any individual who has comprehension of lead pipes concurs leads and benefits remain forever inseparable. More leads implies

more the likelihood of change accordingly leadinv to benefits. So your lead must pipe ought to never dry out.

4. **Leads diminish costing**: Lead age is a mutually beneficial arrangement for both the purchaser and dealer. For instance, purchasers can demand data from a few organizations that offer the item or administration that they are keen on. Then, at that point, the merchant can make their pitch to individuals who have given their authorization. These are the absolute most sweltering leads. Change rates on leads got in this manner are more effective than cold contacts.

These are a portion of the motivations behind why you ought to have a sound lead pipe
In the present exceptionally serious business scene, producing leads is essential for the achievement and development of any organization. Lead age is the most common way of drawing in and catching expected clients or clients who have shown interest in your item or administration. These people, known as leads, are the backbone of any business as they drive deals and income. In this far reaching guide, we will investigate the significance of lead age for business achievement and examine different procedures and best practices that can assist you with creating excellent leads.

Lead age is the first move toward quite a while channel and includes distinguishing expected clients and starting client interest in your items or administrations. A proactive methodology permits organizations to interface with possibilities and convert them into paying clients. The objective of lead age is to catch the contact data of possible leads, for example, their name, email address, or telephone number, so you can support and circle back to them.

Lead age should be possible through different channels, including on the web and disconnected strategies. **Online lead** age methods include utilizing advanced advertising systems like site improvement (Web optimization), content promoting, virtual entertainment showcasing, and email advertising. **Disconnected lead** age procedures, then again, may incorporate customary promoting techniques like print advertisements, radio, or regular postal mail. Lead age assumes an urgent part in the outcome of any business. The fuel drives deals and income, permitting organizations to develop and flourish.

Here are a few key motivations behind why lead age is fundamental for business achievement:

1. **Expanded Deals Open doors**: Lead age furnishes organizations with a constant flow of qualified leads, expanding the possibilities changing over them into paying clients. By focusing on people who have proactively shown interest in your item or administration, you can altogether build your deals open doors.

2. **savvy showcasing:** Lead age is a practical promoting methodology contrasted with other conventional publicizing techniques. Rather than burning through a lot of cash on mass promoting efforts, organizations can zero in their endeavors on focusing on unambiguous crowds who are bound to change over into clients.

3. **More noteworthy Profit** from Speculation (return on initial capital investment): With legitimate lead age methodologies set up, organizations can accomplish a better yield on venture. By producing quality leads and sustaining them through the deals channel, organizations can change over leads into clients and drive income development.

4. **further developed Client commitment:** lead age permits organizations to draw in with possible clients at a beginning phase. By catching their contact data, you can tailor your showcasing messages and give customized encounters, expanding client commitment and devotion.

5. **Market Development**: Lead age empowers organizations to extend their range and target new business sectors. By recognizing potential clients who may not know about your image, you can acquaint yourself with your items or administrations with a more extensive crowd and tap into new market sections.

6. **Upper hand**: In the present serious business scene, lead age gives you a strategic advantage. By successfully catching leads, sustaining connections, and changing over them into clients, you can outflank your rivals and set up a good foundation for yourself as a market chief.

In view of these advantages, obviously compelling lead age is fundamental for business achievement. By executing the right procedures and methods, organizations can create a predictable progression of qualified leads and drive deals development.

- **Know Where Your Objective Market Invests Energy On the web**

To start with, you really want to know where your objective market is and where they visit regularly. In the past times, it would be an actual area. Today, it's a virtual area. Is it safe to say that they are on Facebook or LinkedIn? What sites do they visit? When you realize their home bases, you can limit your promoting to focus on those particular destinations, areas or distributions

- **Influence Web-based Entertainment Hashtags**

It sounds peculiar, however I hosted a third get-together produce a hashtag list for me. The hashtags were applicable to the clients I was trying to draw in. I observed that each post was arriving at additional possible clients, rather than me simply dropping data with my fingers crossed. Hashtags can be key and designated, offering an incredible method for utilizing your ongoing online entertainment openness and draw in new clients. -

- **Request Tributes**

One of the most outstanding ways of producing drives is to request them. Tribute promoting through informal (up close and personal communication) is the most significant type of advertising. Requesting that your clients share the work you accomplish for themselves and the worth it brings to their business is an extraordinary method for creating leads. Begin requesting that your clients allude names of individuals they realize who could profit from your administrations.

- **Converse with Your Optimal Clients About Your Contribution**

Join the cutting edge (innovation) with the ageless (association). Prior to sending off another program or administration, ponder five ideal clients you might want to work with. Connect and simply have a virtual discussion with them about your contribution: How often seven days could they preferably like it? What amount could they feel open to money management? How long could they favor the length to be?

- **Get Perfectly clear On Your Image Story**

The simplest method for removing the pressure from managing evolving calculations,
refreshes on stages, apparatuses traveling every which way and contrasting yourself with your opposition is to become perfectly clear about your mystery ingredient (also known as your image). What's your story? What worth might you at any point give? How would you make it happen? Who benefits the most from it? That reality is, your story is the main thing nobody can rival. A task should be possible by anybody.

- **Make Your Computerized Impression**

Making your computerized impression is a complex method for producing leads. This incorporates utilizing virtual entertainment channels, making content, for example, assessment pieces, thought initiative and remarks on outsider posts, drawing in with the right center gatherings through hashtags, increasing your validity through different affiliations, enrollments and associations — the rundown can be a long one. Draw an activity plan and put it all on the line.

- **Direct A LinkedIn Lead Program**

I think it truly relies upon the business you are in and furthermore the speed at which you really want to transform leads into deals. For a more extended game, I would propose utilizing content promoting, as this will bring individuals into your channel by conveying esteem, possibly prompting deals in the long haul. In any case, online is where everything is occurring right now, so I would take a gander at directing a LinkedIn lead program.

- **Make Worth Based, Human-Centered Content**

Make esteem based, human-centered content in different mediums in light of your one of a kind purchaser's excursion. Organizations invest a great deal a lot of energy being item engaged in their substance and insufficient time relating their items with how a client's concerns can be fixed. By adopting a worth based strategy to content promoting, organizations will actually want to connect the trust hole and abbreviate the deals cycle

- **Approach Fulfilled Clients For References**

Your most ideal way of finding incredible leads is generally references from fulfilled clients.

Don't hesitate for even a moment to ask these people for their thoughts or for video tributes, which you can put on your site or in short email joins. Nothing is preferable for business over having cheerful clients discuss you and recount stories that will resound with your possibilities

- **Lead From A Position Of Enthusiasm**

How would you draw in the people who might esteem having a relationship with you? Most will lead with a deals mentality. To separate yourself, begin with understanding your "why" and lead enthusiastically for what you can add to an association. At the point when you lead from a position of enthusiasm, it will be acknowledged as veritable and can prompt confided in connections.

- **Center Around Conveying Separated Worth**

"Go-providers" get more. The best leads are the ones that your ongoing clients proactively create for you. In this manner, an emphasis on ensuring your clients gain separated worth will be the way to producing leads at the least expense.

- **Have Instructive Online courses**

Online courses are awesome, "one-to-many" advertising vehicles that permit you to share thoughts, instruct and show your expertise for your interest group. The people who click on your greeting have an interest in your subject; the people who go to probably have a genuine need deserve follow-up. What's more, online class solicitations emailed and web-based entertainment likewise act as extraordinary marking instruments.

Estimating and Following Lead Age Achievement

promoting, or paid publicizing, you can dispense your assets to the best channels and enhance your lead age endeavors.

- **Time-to-Transformation**:

Estimating the time it takes for a lead to change over into a client is significant for surveying the effectiveness of your lead sustaining process. By following the time it takes for prompts travel through the deals pipe, you can recognize bottlenecks, upgrade your lead supporting procedures, and abbreviate the deals cycle.

- **Model**:

A product as-a-administration (SaaS) organization can follow the quantity of site guests, the level of guests who pursue a free preliminary, and the level of preliminary clients who convert into paying clients. By investigating these measurements, they can distinguish the best lead age channels, advance their site transformation rate, and work on their preliminary to-client change rate.

By routinely checking and examining these measurements, you can acquire important experiences into the presentation of your lead age endeavors and pursue information driven choices to work on your outcomes. It is vital to lay out clear objectives and benchmarks for every measurement and track them reliably after some time to assess the adequacy of your lead age methodologies.

Lead Age Best Practices for B2B Organizations

can examine lead information to distinguish the best lead age channels or missions. By allotting their assets to the best techniques, they can enhance their lead age endeavors and produce more excellent leads.

By carrying out these prescribed procedures, B2B organizations can improve their lead age endeavors and draw in high-esteem clients. It is critical to continually assess and refine your systems in view of market patterns, client input, and information examination to remain in front of the opposition.

Chapter 5

Supporting Leads

While you're seeking clients on the web, each lead counts. That implies each time somebody gives you their contact data or collaborates with your site, you want to move them through the deals channel rapidly and transform them into a paying client. That development is designated "lead sustaining," and it's one of the most mind-blowing approaches to ceaselessly create new clients for your business on the web.

Business-to-business (B2B) organizations frequently use lead sustaining to drive deals home, thus carry on with work to-customer (B2C) organizations that proposition significant buys like vehicles or houses. Lead sustaining or supporting leads, nonetheless, is for each organization — even the ones that blossom with fast exchanges like online business stores.

What is supporting lead
Lead sustaining is the most common way of laying out and assembling associations with leads (or expected clients) all through the purchaser venture. A lead sustaining procedure can utilize a few channels and promoting strategies, including email, virtual entertainment, and publicizing.
Lead sustaining is intended to complete two things: Convert leads and distinguish areas of progress for your deals channel. Both of these are fundamental since one gives you a real client and different assists you with getting more clients later.

At the point when you meet both of these targets for sustaining leads, you open enormous development potential for your business, and you can arrive at your lead supporting advertising objectives

Let's take a look at each step of the lead nurturing process.

- **Lead Age**

Your business offers an impetus to the commercial center. Anybody who takes you up on this proposition — for example, downloading content or finishing up a structure — demonstrates an interest in your organization. This is trailed by a thank you for answering the source of inspiration.

- **Approval**

Certain individuals who answer a lead age message are genuinely intrigued by the organization's items or administrations. Others are simply intrigued by free stuff. Here your business isolates one class of possibilities from the other.

- **Commitment**

When a lead has been qualified, now is the ideal time to connect and extend the discussion. This could be a call, online overview or other data gathering correspondence. It could likewise be a course of instructing the lead on answers for their requirements. One way or the other, it's expected to sustain the lead and spur a buy.

- Transformation

This stage starts when the possibility is prepared to pull the trigger and purchase. The individual might answer a source of inspiration during the commitment stage or connect and start the exchange. The outcome is another deal — and another client.

The lead age and sustaining process sounds adequately basic, yet it's not. The whole cycle relies upon your capacity to connect with a message so convincing and significant that the possibility goes flawlessly starting with one phase then onto the next.

Step by step instructions to construct a cutthroat supporting lead technique

Showcasing supportimg lead is a long cycle, and that implies everything needs to go right in the event that a lead will turn into a client. Your lead supporting procedure will be modified to your specific business and industry, however it has the most obvious opportunity with regards to progress in the event that it depends on these three major advances:

- No two clients are precisely similar, yet a few possibilities are more reasonable for your organization than others. They might live in a specific piece of the nation, come from a specific foundation, or have a specific arrangement of individual or expert requirements. Fabricate a profile of your objective client, and you'll have a superior possibility picking the right leads for your sustaining effort.

    Investigate clients who have bought comparable items and administrations. How old would they say they are? What kind of work do they do? What requirements were met by their buys? Utilize these subtleties to figure out who might be generally inspired by your ongoing deal, and watch out for new leads that fit that profile.

You can utilize this data, for instance, to send lobbies for:

a. Enlistment
b. Occasional advancements
c. Re-commitment
d. Occasion advancements
    From there, the sky is the limit

2. Make a correspondence plan

As leads go through your lead supporting methodology, they need to hear various messages before they advance to the following stage. The objective of these message ought to be twofold:
1: To guarantee them of the legitimacy of your deal,
2: To buiild their inspiration to buy. Foster interchanges for each phase of the supporting system that accomplish both.

The purchasing cycle can give you signs on this.
The mindfulness stage ought to incorporate a fast introduction of your business or deal, alongside an encouragement to find out more. The thought stage ought to go further, offering motivations to purchase the item and pick your organization over others. A few leads will go directly to the purchasing stage. Those that won't require an extra motivator or confirmation before they close the arrangement.

3. Take on a CRM approach
Client relationship the executives guarantees organizations are drawing in with clients such that causes the client to feel esteemed and appreciated. Rather than hearing a standard pitch about another item, the client catches wind of modified arrangements and exceptionally designated items fit to their requirements.

Remember this thought creating your supporting lead
In the beginning phases of lead supporting, CRM seems to be division, where potential leads are drawn nearer with what could intrigue them. As you go further into the cycle, these collaborations can be more customized to reflect what every individual possibility is searching for from your organization.

This approach will assist you with understanding the inclinations of your objective market, which will build the possibilities changing over additional leads into clients.

For instance, you can utilize this information to send post-buy messages that recommend:
- Posting a survey
- Booking a subsequent help
- Making a subsequent buy
- At the point when you sustain a lead, you're truly fabricating a relationship. Likewise with some other relationship, the right move can prompt a lifetime responsibility, while some unacceptable move could cause an extremely durable break. Get your lead supporting showcasing and lead advertising

methodology process down, so you generally know what to say and when to say it.

The Lead Suppo

Chapter 6

Sales Conversion

The conversion of a prospect to lead and lead to a customer is termed as Sales Conversion.

A possibility is a potential future client who is keen on knowing your item or administration. Prospect could conceivably change over completely to a lead and in the event that not sought after as expected, the possibility might be lost or switched over completely to rivalry. Possibilities are the primary phase of the Deals and they ought to be persistently sought after. In any case, the correspondence that is saved for possibilities ought to be early on and gentle as opposed to consistent barraging. The inconspicuous correspondence doesn't drive off the possibility and as time goes, the possibility converts to a lead.

Lead is a positive possibility. The person who has consented to be a potential purchaser can be named as lead. In any case, it depends on the sales rep to time-bound the lead and create the deal. A lead is to be conveyed successfully and the deals calls are to be finished with the goal of tending to the requirements and needs of the client. A forceful scrutiny of lead is basic in order to switch it over completely to a client.

New client is one who has not bought the administrations or results of the organization of all time. On the off chance that the client is utilizing contender items and, chooses to go with your items, he would be named as ***contender transformation***. It might likewise be conceivable that the client is totally new and has not utilized the opposition at any point yet is beginning with your items. All things considered, some term them as ***New Client***

Contender transformation When a client is utilizing rivalry items or administrations and converts to your items, it would be named as ***contender change***. You want to keep a severe watch on the number of contenders deals exercises are giving transformations and furthermore contenders deals changes rates.

Client overhaul at the point when a client changes from fundamental results of an organization to premium results of a similar organization, it will be known as client update or higher transformation. A few organizations might think about this as new change or new client for that specific item.

The Business change might be new or existing who moves up to high-esteem section or a contender deals transformation. In both cases, the client is to be followed up right from the underlying phase of prospect till transformation. There is a cycle for change of offer which is known as ***Deals Channel.***

Deals Pipe is an incredible instrument to concentrate on the course of Deals transformation. It is the method involved with switching a possibility over completely to a client by filtering through the whole populace and by following the interaction.

The Following are the means for Deals transformation:

Mindfulness: As the terms propose, the populace ought to be made mindful of the items that the dealer has. It very well may be through a media that mindfulness should be possible however without mindfulness, the populace can not be aware of the contributions and until they know, they won't buy. Subsequently making clients mindful by advertisements or some other specialized strategies is significant.

Interest: The second phase of Deals Change is intriguing. The ones that become intrigued after a mindfulness crusade express their advantage. In certain ventures, the salesman needs to produce interest in the personalities of the client by posing appropriate shut finished inquiries. It is vital that at this stage, there ought to be the utilization of shut finished questions as opposed to inquiries without a right or wrong answer since this stage chooses if the possibility is to be followed up or not. Posing a shut finished inquiry during a deals call or in interest structure will let the goals of the client plainly to the dealer.

Independent direction: Here comes into the image the abilities of the sales rep. A legitimate opening of the Deals call, having appropriate targets close by, time-bound activities to relieve any questions in the personalities of client and giving item demos are to be done appropriately and proficiently by the salesman. Persuading abilities are of critical significance at this stage since in the event that the lead isn't persuaded, the organization would lose a likely client.

Activity: When the choice is positive, the deal will occur and in the event that the choice is negative, the lead will be lost or cold lead. The activity stage is where the choice is set in motion.

Illustration of Deals Change
To outline this cycle lets take a model. While perusing online entertainment, you coincidentally find an advertisement of another iPad Genius 12.9 inch. You click the promotion, watch it yet close it later saying the item is excessively costly. Toward the finish of a promotion, there is a review structure about the advertisement which you fill and which likewise asks your contact subtleties.

Later you get a call from Apple store inquiring as to whether you have as of late perused their promotion, to which you answer emphatically. *This is where you become a possibility*. The apple store welcomes you to descend at a predefined time to examine more the proposals to which you concur. This is the interest stage. You go down the store and converse with the Deals master who makes sense of you the elements, benefits lastly gives you an adaptable funding choice consequently eliminating your obstaclw.

Presently as a piece of the activity, you pay the primary check and the deal is shut. On the off chance that you were utilizing a Microsoft surface and have changed to iPad, it would be contender transformation and assuming you have never utilized a tablet, it would be another deals change. By seeking after these stages, one can change over the possibilities and cut them down the business pipe to accomplish deals transformation.

Significance of deals change

I. Higher income age for the organization inferable from expanded and new deals.

ii. Expanded item profundity and afterward broadness. For instance, an underlying client of Tide cleanser begins utilizing other Delegate and Bet items.

iii. Expanded prospective customer to higher piece of the pie.

Following the deals channel, the organization can monitor the current status of the imminent clients and leads and configuration advertising systems likewise

Chapter 7

Increasing customer lifetime value

What Is Client Lifetime Worth?
Here is the most straightforward client lifetime esteem definition - a measurement demonstrates the way that much net benefit your organization can make of one client over the long haul.

In this way, a high CLV method every client will get more income for your organization. Since every client turns out to be more important, it implies your organization can stand to spend more to obtain new clients and hold the current ones.

Suppose you run a work of art, unadulterated play SaaS administration with month to month charging. We will involve a solitary client for instance, one who stays with your business for quite some time, and who got a membership plan valued at $100/month.
The typical client lifetime worth of that client would be $2,400 ($100 times 24 - the quantity of months that individual has been a client). That number just gets higher as the client will pay more over the long run, the extension income from existing clients surpassing the stir.

Client Lifetime Worth Recipe
For additional important experiences, client lifetime esteem estimation ought to be finished utilizing both: a typical income and a typical benefit. Each can give significant information on how clients are answering your item and how to change your advertising endeavors effectively.

How to Expand Client Lifetime Worth?
Expanding your CLV can be all around as straightforward as exchanging your charging cycle from month to month to yearly, or as intense as redesiging your

client care process. Beneath, we've recorded 14 demonstrated strategies to expand your normal CLV and produce additional income from your current clients.

1. Further develop the Onboarding System
With regards to Client Achievement, onboarding is the cycle you ought to pull out all the stops on to guarantee reasonable business development. It ought to be among the first concerns as poor onboarding happens to be the main source of agitate, 23% to be more unambiguous.

It's here that your client truly draws in with your item and where you can have the best constructive outcome. This being said, it's critical to assemble a vital onboarding interaction to support new clients returning for more, and consequently increment their lifetime worth to your organization.
The interaction can be unique, contingent upon the business, client needs or wanted results. In any case, there are a couple of key tips that most organizations use to connect with their crowd and increment reception.
As a matter of some importance, one should make the onboarding as simple and quick as could really be expected. This should be possible by working on the cycle with walkthrough guides, intelligent how-to recordings, wrapped instructional exercises and other substance that could be useful to clients in satisfying their objectives.

Consider customizing the onboarding grouping by fitting it to the purchaser persona. Center around imparting the worth of your contribution right all along. Test onboarding approaches and screen the client wellbeing score in view of their way of behaving.
Anything that choice you go for, ensure it is adequately clear to be perceived and supports commitment.

2. Offer some benefit Pressed Content That Keeps Clients Locked in
Email showcasing is one of the most mind-blowing ways of holding clients, yet numerous organizations go about it the incorrect way. Rather than sending esteem pressed content, they run mechanized dribble crusades without offering any worth.

The best kind of messages to ship off your clients are the ones that stress your item/administration esteem:

Assuming you give bookkeeping administrations, send a week by week or month to month email let clients know how much cash you've assisted them with saving that month;

In the event that you give assistance work area programming, send a month to month email to clients illuminating them the number of help tickets they effectively tackled;

On the off chance that you sell a harmless to the ecosystem item, email your clients to let them know how substantially less carbon dioxide they've delivered by utilizing a contending item.

Each item or administration conveys esteem. The way in to a successful message is to track down that worth and present it to your clients such that shows your commitment. An email that makes sense of the advantages you get goes much further - according to a CLV point of view - than another limited time email.

One more means to be taken up is instructive substance. This sort of message depends on the customized sharing of information. The key here is customized. This is the second when you want to dispose of deals pitches, investigate explicit client needs, and recommend ways of tackling their concerns utilizing your administration/item.

Your principal objective is to plan the client venture, recognize the touchpoints, and, on this ground, convey profoundly designated customized missions to make yourself noticeable as a dependable wellspring of information. Show up for your clients, consistently prepared to help, and they will compensate you appropriately.

3. **Offer Very good quality Client support**

Quality client support is a vital venture to help your business develop and increment maintenance. Assuming that your administration is sub optimal, clients will abscond to contenders regardless of whether your item is better than expected. Information uncovers that 33% of shoppers are probably going to switch brands after a solitary occurrence of unfortunate client support.

In that capacity, it's essential to get client assistance right. Better client support rises to a superior client experience. Thusly, that will make your current clients bound to become steadfast long haul clients.

Yet, how would you offer first rate client assistance that helps client maintenance and increments client lifetime esteem? Indeed, the following are a couple of suggestions you ought to consider:

- *Offer Omni-Channel Backing*

As a business, being dynamic on however many channels as could reasonably be expected is significant. Cross-channel connections represents a huge effect on client maintenance (58%) and support (55%).

The vast majority own more than one gadget - in the US alone, 98% of individuals switch between gadgets consistently. Also that around 66% of clients use something like 3 different correspondence channels to contact support.

In a perfect world, you ought to investigate which channels your clients utilize the most. Perhaps they're more dynamic on Wire and Twitter while you just proposition email and telephone support. When you know, ensure your help group is appropriately prepared in utilizing that large number of channels, or - assuming cash permits it - set up various groups answerable for each channel.

Give day in and day out Help. No mystery individuals (be they B2C or business purchasers) anticipate that a quick reaction should their inquiries and backing demands. One of the most incredible ways of offering that is through nonstop client assistance. While it's costly, it's likewise worth the effort. However, on the off chance that you can't give all day, every day support, ensure your group can answer as quick as conceivable to client demands.

Furthermore, obviously, in the event that you can offer all day, every day support, you ought to in any case teach your group to answer client tickets as quick as possible. Remember - clients will be particularly anticipating that for this situation.

In general, you ought to ensure you have a thoroughly prepared, responsive, and devoted help group for the most traffic-weighty channels.

- <u>Screen Virtual Entertainment</u>

At the point when clients connect via virtual entertainment, be it to request backing or leave an objection, they're doing it most importantly in light of the fact that they anticipate a quick reaction.

The way things are, roughly 84% of customers anticipate a reaction in the span of 24 hours on the off chance that they post grievances via web-based entertainment.

On Twitter, things are significantly more tense, as 72% of individuals anticipate a reaction soon.

On the off chance that they don't get a convenient reaction, clients will in all probability impart their disappointment to your image to companions via web-based entertainment. Stages like Facebook make it much more straightforward for them to screen your typical reaction time.

As per writer and writer Emily Yellin, in the past when a call to an organization turned sour, clients would tell their family and perhaps their colleagues, yet no other individual. Presently everyone can see those discussions - making the stakes rather high.

Remembering the dangers, your group should have somewhere around one representative zeroed in on following and answering to virtual entertainment remarks. Focusing on those objections would be a decent beginning

- *Offer Live Talk Backing*

Around 80% of business purchasers believe that organizations should answer and associate with them continuously. The most effective way to offer them that is through live talk - client-organization correspondences that occur progressively on the organization's site or application.

The measurements don't lie - live visit is very valuable for organizations. Around 79% of clients say they favor utilizing live visit since it offers prompt reactions. Additionally, site guests who utilize live visit on your site are worth 4.5 times more than the ones who don't, so there's a lot of space to increment changes with them.

Additionally, live talk permits working remotely which makes it more straightforward for your group to give day in and day out help.

- *Keep an Information Base*

An Information Base is a significant piece of your help foundation where you should offer admittance to self-administration articles, instructional exercises, video guides, and other supporting documentation. While assembling one will take some time, exertion, and cash, everything will work out just fine.

As per research, around 91% of shoppers would prefer to utilize an Information Base in the event that it is accessible, and 70% of them like to utilize an organization's site to tackle their concerns as opposed to utilizing email or telephone support.

Moreover, an information base will ease the heat off your help group. For example, a client can be consequently diverted to an important information base article or instructional exercise when they present a solicitation (or even before they make it happen), utilizing robotized bots. This could keep said client cheerful by offering them a speedy arrangement or reply, while permitting your help group to deal with other, possibly more pressing help tickets.

Chatbots become more well known these days as they permit organizations to help clients every minute of every day without utilizing an extra human labor force. Designed appropriately, they will assist clients with getting arrangements faster than customary strategies for client care. While the greater part actually favors human connection, 40% say it doesn't matter at all to them whether they converse with a device or a genuine individual as long as their concern is tackled. Many organizations use chatbots effectively on their sites, however on Facebook also.

4. Fabricate Connections

Cultivating great client connections is basic to the continuous outcome of your business, powerless connections representing 16% of the typical client agitate.

All through the client venture and during every one of your connections with a client, sustaining a solid bond is significant. The key is to cause them to feel tuned in and appreciated, realizing they're managing a proactive and proficient group.

Dale Carnegie said: "You can make more companions in two months by becoming keen on others than you can in two years by attempting to get others inspired by you." While he was looking at making companions, a similar standard applies to the business world.

- Get to understand your listeners' perspective and tap into their sentiments and assumptions. Studying your clients would furnish you with a modest bunch of bits of knowledge in this regard, assisting you with bettering follow through on your commitments. Be proactive and screen client wellbeing by interfacing with your crowd consistently and not just when you have something to sell. Keeping a heartbeat on consumer loyalty will likewise permit you to make a prompt move if there should be an occurrence of an unexpected reduction.

- Give appropriate consideration to building associations with the top portions of your client base, key contacts, and leader staff. Direct quarterly business audits to ensure you are in total agreement and request criticism on existing cycles and on what's coming straightaway. Cause them to feel allowed with the singular consideration they merit.

5. Pay attention to Your Clients - Gather Noteworthy Criticism

Blissful clients are steadfast clients. Developing your business without realizing your clients' thought process of you is incredibly difficult. Developing with itemized, noteworthy criticism, then again, is a far simpler cycle.

- Understanding your clients allows you to focus on the parts of your business that fuel consumer loyalty and income development, all while downsizing ineffectual strategies. It additionally gives genuine information on how likely your current clients are to prescribe your item or administration to their companions.

You ought to gather and store all the criticism you get in one spot and offer it across divisions. Likewise, have a group that is answerable for observing client opinion on the web (via virtual entertainment, correspondence channels, survey sites, and so on.).

- Convey consumer loyalty overviews - NPS and CSAT. We suggest NPS over CSAT, a one-question review that asks on the probability of proposal to companions or partners on a 0-10 scale. In light of the got criticism, the respondents are portioned into three classifications: Advertisers are your 9 and 10s, Passives go for 7 and 8 and Naysayers range between 0 to 6. You can ascertain your NPS score by deducting the level of Doubters from the level of Advertisers. NPS makes it simple to evaluate client joy and permits you to send follow-up inquiries to figure out what precisely clients love or disdain about your business, and what enhancements they might want to see.

A high NPS score assists you with expanding your CLV since cheerful clients are definitely bound to remain with your business than miserable ones. Zeroing in on expanding your NPS is an extraordinary method for keeping your stir rate low while extending your client base.

With regards to effectively gathering client criticism, utilizing specific NPS programming is an answer worth considering. These instruments are embraced by numerous organizations to simpler forestall beat, increment development, and oversee more clients with less exertion.

Particular NPS programming is a phenomenal means to save time and get a reasonable perspective on your clients, since it coordinates with different administrations you as of now use, as CRM and help work area programming. Furthermore, it gathers and gives admittance to helpful client information and high level revealing in one spot.

With everything taken into account, NPS programming is an extraordinary method for easing the heat off your client achievement and backing groups, permitting them to more readily zero in on further developing the client experience. Basically, they'll have the option to diminish beat levels, enhance the client lifecycle, improve onboarding and long haul client relationship, increment reestablishment rates, and subsequently drive more benefit.

6. Identify Normal Trouble spots and Give Arrangements

The thought is to investigate your clients' input, and recognize the most incessant repeating issues that are being accounted for.

NPS reviews make this undertaking truly straightforward, permitting you to gather significant input and identify normal trouble spots for the two Naysayers, clients who are not content with your image, and Passives, clients who like your image, however insufficient to turn into an Advertiser.

When the most applicable objections are recognized, these must be focused on relying upon the recurrence of event. Another methodology is focus on the issues that cross-over with the two Passives and Doubters.

On the off chance that the criticism is too unclear to ever be matched, attempt to bunch it into classifications, with respect to model "accelerate support answers" or "smooth out onboarding process".

When the issues are distinguished and focused on, the proper divisions should be educated and conceded full admittance to the required information, in an open organization. Obviously, the need to get moving in fixing these issues is an unquestionable requirement.

7. Offer Your Clients a Customized Insight

Administration, item, and experience personalization are foremost these days in the event that you maintain that clients should be cheerful and spend more on your business over the long haul. All things considered, 81% of customers say they anticipate that organizations should both comprehend them and know when the perfect opportunity and second to move toward them is.

Likewise, around 77% of buyers have clearly spent more cash on or suggested a brand that has offered a customized administration or experience.

B2B purchasers certainly need a more customized insight, and a big part of the US B2B advertisers who attempted site personalization said it was powerful.

The following are two or three different ways personalization can assist you with upgrading your client lifetime esteem over the long haul:

With regards to B2B purchasers, personalization can assist you with conveying your messages through the perfect channel at the ideal time. Those things don't simply represent the deciding moment an arrangement - they likewise decide if a client turns into a recurrent purchaser.

- By getting to realize your clients better, you can fundamentally further develop the onboarding system by causing it to feel significantly more "natural" and inviting to new clients.
- Personalization can assist your item with conveying a superior client experience with a more instinctive UI. Furthermore, its an obvious fact that 8 of every 10 customers will pay more cash for a superior encounter. Also that an interest in UX/UI can return a good return on initial capital investment.

- You can utilize personalization to make profoundly customized in-application messages for every client portion you have, expanding your chances of changing over clients with a lower-paid plan to a more generously compensated membership.

With a superior comprehension of what your clients need, how they feel, and what their identity is, it becomes simpler to perform strategically pitching and upselling. Personalization assists you with conveying better and more significant client service, which is crucial to increment client esteem over the long haul. It likewise causes it more straightforward for clients to feel like they have a genuine connection with your image, rather than simply being a wellspring of benefit.

How can you offer revenue-boosting personalization?

It's pretty much a mix of researching relevant customer data in-depth (which is much easier if you follow the advice we offer at #8) and collecting, analyzing, and acting on customer feedback (this is where NPS surveys help a lot).

8. Share your Item Guide

An item guide is an extensively planned layout of an item presenting throughout a stretch of time - an assertion of purpose that matches the means connected with an item's turn of events. It's one more wellspring of inspiration and proprietorship imparting to colleagues.

Nearly everything on the item guide has an objective that plans to meet the necessities of the group and those of the clients. Thus, the item guide isn't exclusively an inside methodology guide and an arrangement for execution, yet in addition a responsibility towards client objectives, making it essential to be shared both inside and remotely.

Inside guides are revolved around features/fixes, conveyance and accomplishments. They are overall more granular giving more careful nuances and courses of occasions.

The work a person from the gathering does commonly looks at inside a construction, thusly offering the thing guide helps to changing your gathering and their necessities, as well as make energy for a thing philosophy.

Other than allowing the gathering to be in complete understanding and act in a comparative course, imparting the advisers for your clients is a fair technique offering clients an unrivaled cognizance of the thing, the components to be consolidated (especially if the different part is a gigantic issue) and the associated plan. Figuring out the regular worth of a thing's components and its motivator for a client is essential.

Specialists can share the thing guide with clients as an element of closing a comprehension or building interest. Client Accomplishment gatherings - being more based on offering responses for existing issues and offering execution improvement - can share advisers for let clients know that it integrates a solution for a continuous deterrent or a getting together with a relevant stage. Taking into account client input reliably and incorporating it into your thing guide will undeniably impact your client lifetime regard, keeping client premium alarm and making things that are redone to client needs.

While sharing thing advisers for conceivable outcomes or existing clients, these should be by and large based on their benefit. It's judicious to do whatever it takes not to put precise dates on somewhat available aides aside from assuming that there is clear conviction. A thing guide is a work in progress so giving a check as opposed to express dates would be great. Better to stay moderate yet to surpass assumptions

Amazon has culminated upselling and strategically pitching and uses the two practices to drive a gigantic measure of extra income consistently. Utilized appropriately, upselling and strategically pitching might both assist you at any point with creating an extra 10% or more income each month from your current clients.

Here are a few incredible tips for strategically pitching and upselling to your ongoing clients:

Offer pack items: Gather various items and administrations and sell them at a lower cost than what they would have been sold for independently. It assists you with expanding the worth of client buys by offering reciprocal items in a combo.

- Offer brief redesigns: This turns out best for SaaS organizations. Take a stab at giving clients who have a fundamental membership a free impermanent (7-day or 14-day) move up to your top notch plan after an update. A few clients may be able to completely make that change once they get to see what your more costly memberships bring to the table direct.
- Utilize a sidebar gadget with famous decisions: You can have a little rundown of well known items on your sidebar. This permits your clients to see the most well known items when they are perusing your site
- Add reciprocal items at checkout: Items you offer as strategically pitches ought to address the requirements of your client. Preferably, they ought to supplement the essential item in the shopping basket.

- Free delivery with least spend: "free" without anyone else energizes numerous purchasers, yet when you consolidate it with free transportation with a base request size condition, it makes it much seriously engaging. Clients are bound to spend more cash - that they would have in any case spent on transportation - to purchase something different.

- Keep proposals restricted: Don't overpower possible clients with an excessive number of decisions. In any case, you risk clients leaving the truck. When confronted with a decision, it's simpler for clients to settle on three things than ten.

9. Execute a Dunning The executives Framework

A dunning the executives framework is an answer that naturally retries a bombed installment or terminated Mastercard and sends a dribble of reestablishment notices to clients at whatever point a charge to their Visa is declined. It ends up being critical for any membership business, forestalling disappointment and disturbance driven client agitate.

All things considered, Mastercard charges can fall flat for various reasons:

- Charge card limits
- Prohibitive corporate cost approaches
- Terminated Mastercards

- Taken Visas
- Lost Visas

Freezing a client's record too quick in such a circumstance can adversely affect the experience they have with your organization. Obviously, in the event that you're excessively merciful with declined charges, your business will likewise need to endure since you'll simply wind up losing cash over the long haul.

Besides, dunning the board can bring down your agitate rate and further develop your client lifetime esteem by empowering programmed charge retries. Along these lines, accounts are not shut rashly since you can charge the card again several days prior to the record ought to be shut, for instance.

Also, this arrangement tells clients precisely when the help can be reestablished once more. Numerous clients would probably see the value in this sort of update since it saves them time as they don't have to look into your FAQ segment or contact your help group by email or telephone.

Also, a dunning management system ensures you won't have to deal with so many angry emails or calls from upset customers who forgot they had your service or product set to autopay. Sure, that won't necessarily do wonders for your CLV rates directly, but it will reduce your brand's odds of getting negative reviews because of it.

And, of course, the automation offered by dunning management saves your support plenty of time. They don't need to waste hours on counter-checking and sending out dozens of reminders and follow-ups. Instead, they can focus on other tasks.

Here are some billing management systems with incorporated dunning management functions:
- Chargify
- Recurly
- Chargebee
- Paddle

10. Run Loyalty Programs

Ensuring customer retention and as a result a higher customer lifetime value can also be accomplished with the help of loyalty programs which offer incentives for repeat business. This can include offering discounts or rewards, by means of loyalty cards, setting up loyalty apps or points schemes to earn on purchases. These programs can be very successful if they are properly implemented.

Among the most natural models are the carriers that offer miles relying upon the ticket admission. Successive fliers like to utilize a similar carrier to gather miles and get a free ticket. The beauty care products brand Tarte rewards focuses for buys, however for filled-in overviews and commitment via virtual entertainment.

You could likewise attempt the allude a-companion methodology: Airbnb program permits visitors to get rewards for each alluded companion who books a condo. However, that is not all: Airbnb urges visitors to spend the obtained reward as it has a lapse date - provoking them to involve the help too and spend more.

On the off chance that devotion programs don't appear to be feasible to you, reward your clients for each x measure of cash spent or make participation programs that offer extra advantages at a little cost. A genuine model is Amazon Prime: individuals from this program get quicker conveyance - which is what each client needs - and, furthermore, music and video real time. Additionally, as indicated by CIRP, Amazon Prime individuals just get better with time, expanding their spending over years.

You ought to likewise know your most savage Advertisers and award them by means of explicit missions that perceive their faithfulness. It might incorporate top-of-mind benefits in reliability programs, a preorder of unreleased items, admittance to explicit administrations or even a customized card to say thanks. By causing them to feel exceptional you will actually want to develop a reasonable client relationship

11. Increment Your Evaluating

As a business owner it's normal you will need to expand your evaluating as you develop because of different reasons. It very well may be either on the grounds that you changed your client profile, added new elements to further develop your item's abilities that should be adapted or basically in light of the fact that the current costs have not been modified for a really long time and are not productive. Organizations frequently will more often than not undervalue their administrations when they initially begin, all things considered.

Besides, Andreas Hinterhuber's review alludes to evaluating as a to a great extent dismissed device in promoting, a 5% cost increment prompting a 22% improvement in benefits that, as per the creator, is undeniably more than some other techniques.

As far as development, Patrick Campbell, President of Cost Keenly and ProfitWell represents a 30-40% increment in income for organizations that have never sincerely gone after their estimating, and essentially a 11-15% lift for organizations that are more ground breaking.

In any case, what do you do about your current clients? Can we just be look at things objectively for a moment - you can't expect your client maintenance levels to be excessively high in the event that they are shocked with unforeseen charging changes. It's even probably the case some of them could fly off the handle that they could try and leave your image through and through.

To grandstand - in 2010, the administration of Zendesk, the assistance work area programming, shocked clients while raising their costs, bringing about a 300% expansion in month to month expenses for certain clients. Once more, it's normal for organizations to climb charges sooner or later, yet checking how decisively it would influence the bills, particularly of their initial clients, could have stayed away from some unacceptable turns.

That is where granddad charging plans become possibly the most important factor. Basically, you save the first valuing for your current clients, and carry out the new evaluating plans you need for new clients.

Another methodology is give clients a decision and cause them to feel in charge. Give a bunch of choices to existing clients so they have the chance to conclude what suits them better. Suppose, they could have their ongoing arrangement at a higher however limited rate, or minimization it to keep a similar cost.

Along these lines, you get to create more gain while likewise giving existing clients sufficient opportunity to get to adore your image to where they personally will actually want to begin paying something else for your administrations.

12. Impart a Client Driven Approach

Keeping your clients at the core of everything is a significant change that you really want to make while creating and keeping up with associations with potential or existing clients. Organizations which place the client at the core of their association experience expanded client lifetime values as well as diminished turnover.

Building a client driven association requires responsibility. It is basic to focus on the upsides of clients first and impart a client centered thinking into your whole organization. It's anything but a basic popular expression any longer yet rather a critical guideline for business today that can straightforwardly and successfully influence your main concerns.

Organizations should be fixated on making positive encounters for individuals to work on their view of a brand. The whole association should be situated towards its client from administrative center to cutting edge to convey esteem. Organizations need to fabricate a client focused culture, instead of approach it as an oddball exchange.

Bottom line

Assuming you honour your esteem clients, your income will develop. That's all there is to it. It's a question of showing them the amount they mean to your business (by asking them for criticism and following up on it), by offering them precisely what they need (regardless of whether they're not mindful they need it yet) and the greatest possible level of comfort, offering first rate help, and an incredibly customized client experience.

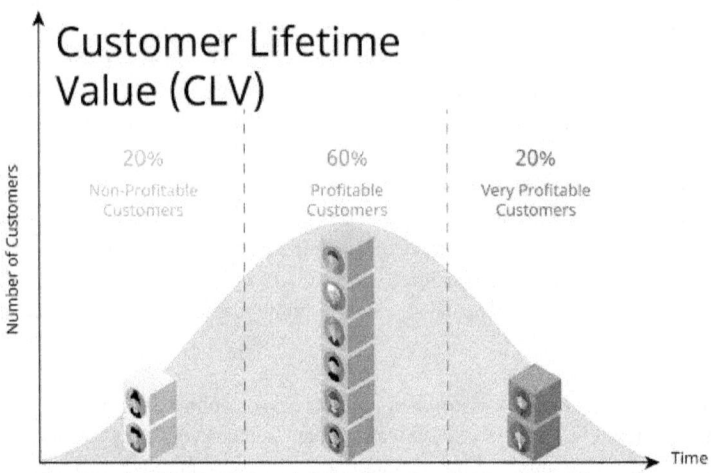

CLV = Average purchase amount × Frequency of purchases × Average Retention Time

Chapter 8

Organizing and animating reference

Do you have at least some idea why clients or possibilities don't make references?

Presenting another relationship too a believed circle is a gamble. Clients have regular apprehension for notoriety harm. It's not unexpected and anticipated.

A sales rep is sitting with his new client. The last "T" is crossed and the keep going "I" dabbed on the agreement. As his new client takes a taste of his espresso the sales rep shares that he'd like a couple of references... . only 100 or so of your dearest companions and clients he says...
His client's eyes lump, and he in a real sense starts to gag on his espresso, he's going paralyzed.
Furthermore, the sales rep expresses out loud whatever? Too much? Alright, what about three or four... . ?

Humor is a great remedy for breaking a possibly off-kilter second. What's more, requesting references can surely qualify as possibly abnormal. This specific line secures the bar ludicrously high and afterward once again introduces at a level so low as to appear to be more than sensible.

Referral /References are one of the most mind-blowing ways of getting more business, as an incredible 84% of individuals trust proposals from individuals they know.

In any case, numerous advertisers swear off reference programs through and through, and the people who have reference programs frequently battle to get them going.

Regardless of whether you have a conventional reference program set up, your business presumably as of now has new clients coming in through verbal exchange showcasing. By investigating these potential open doors, you'll regard yourself as in a mother lode.

All things considered, when somebody comes in as a referral a significant part of the difficult work has previously been finished. Another person, most likely a cheerful client, currently furnished you with believability and a feeling of trust, the two of which are required for making a deal.

Conquering client reference fears.
There are two key feelings of trepidation, *one significant and one minor*, that should be addressed for the client to feel great in giving out a good referral review

Notoriety the executives is the essential hindrance yet how to create a reference can be a test too. You should comprehend that clients and possibilities are unfortunate of giving references.

How might you feel in the event that you alluded a specialist co-op to your closest companion or client and the specialist organization fell all over. Could you be stressed over your standing?

Or on the other hand Envision that you have gone through years constructing an expert connection with somebody who is a forerunner in your field. We should call him John. After some time, major areas of strength for a, regard has developed among you and John. Then, one day you receive an email from an individual you have never met. This individual wants to find out whether you will acquaint him with John, your confided in associate. Could you feel happy with giving a prologue to this irregular individual to John?

Decrease the trepidation
To coordinate your executioner reference technique you should constantly endeavor to diminish, limit or out and out kill client fears. Becauae if for reasons unknown you don't convey your astonishing help, it will ponder severely them. Their standing will be harmed and their confidence will drop. Making a reference is a gamble

Steve Gordon, creator of "Relentless References", declares that dread is the significant explanation that clients don't give you references.

They have great relations with individuals in their circle yet they are continuously behaving irrationally that something could risk their connections. While they accept that you are a fine individual and will work effectively, they are not adequately sure about this to make a reference. The gamble is a lot of lower in the event that they basically neglect to move. thus they do that, and your business loses.

Gordon's answer is basic wipe out completely considered 'deals'. All things considered, think of something that your client can propose to his circle that is so colossally significant that you are presently helping him out instead of the reverse way around.

At the point when you follow through on the reference ... your client will be pleased to have responded your generosity and glad that they could make an exceptional reference to their companion or partner. Up until you convey your administration the outcome is shady. A significant gift eliminates the haze of vulnerability.

Andy Lopata, who has composed three books on systems administration, is considerably more provocative. That's what he says, in many occasions, clients don't give references since they don't believe you should succeed.

This is deep.

Your client believes you should get along nicely and stay in business, however not so well that your business truly takes off and you get droves of clients and he turns out to mean quite a bit to you.

He needs to be dealt with and-at a few level-thinks that this will endure assuming that you are stunningly effective. He won't disrupt you, yet he will take his foot off the gas pedal and he does this by keeping down on references.

Your job is to Console your client, much of the time, that giving references will just build his worth to your organization and that higher worth clients get extra degrees of administration frequently at no extra expense.
The right attitude is basic
Get your reference relationship going on the right foot with the outlook that you are not searching for a deal. You are searching for a prologue to a rich new relationship.

Concentrates on show that just around 7% of the populace is probably going to require your administrations or items right away . Another 10% or so may be convinced that purchasing your items or administration might be significant at that point. Yet, that actually leaves 83% of the populace not prepared or ready to purchase now. At the point when you offer an important gift or administration that your client can be pleased with your let your client know that your essential worth is the presentation.

Your client has to be aware unhesitatingly that you will make every effort to convey a WOW insight to whomever they allude. Offering an endowment of item or administration moves the reference opportunity away from a deals discussion and into a remarkable presentation opportunity

In the event that you are a diamond setter searching for references, you could offer a couple of studs to the alluded prospect. For nothing. Figure how your client will feel in the event that they realize that their reference brought about their companion getting a free sets of studs.

Gifts come in many shapes and sizes it very well may be an endowment of help. You can make this proposal without requesting a reference and it can have a similar outcome.

Here is a basic model: *Mr. Client, assuming that you're ever in a circumstance where somebody you care about needs my assistance, I believe you should know that I'm hanging around for you to have a call and I will assist them in any capacity I with canning. I probably won't have the option to take them on as a client, however we can essentially give them a few direction and assist them with trying not to commit huge errors."*

By doing this with a certifiable expectation to help, you offer a demonstration of administration as opposed to asking your clients for some help. Envision assuming your PCP or attorney offered this assistance. You could be thankful, not horrendously awkward, isn't that so?

Beating How to Make a Reference Dread
The other trepidation, significant yet less testing, is information based. Your client could feel abnormal or under skilled during the time spent making a reference. One idea is to foster a raving fan reference letter. You can set the pattern as a layout and redo it for every client. Your raving fan reference letter gives the client the best words and language structure for conveying the reference either recorded as a hard copy or face to face.

Ensure they realize how best to allude you. Odds are their not incredible at making references, Mentor them through the interaction. Make it as simple as could be expected.

Obviously references ought to be a gigantic concentration for your image. Anyway, how might you get a greater amount of them?

The following are 7 advertising techniques to increment references for your business.

1. *Go above and beyond for endorsers, possibilities, and clients*
Any time somebody connects with your business, they ought to have a decent encounter. At the point when you give extraordinary encounters, individuals pay heed. At the point when individuals pay heed, they will more often than not talk. This discussion causes references.

In this way, assuming you're ready to satisfy a client's necessities, that is perfect. Assuming you're ready to do an amazing job, that is surprisingly better. By doing an amazing job, you put yourself aside from all the clamor that encompasses you. Exceeding everyone's expectations doesn't need to burn through every last cent by the same token. The following are a couple of approaches the additional mile:

- Send conditional messages with certainty
- Send your conditional messages and advertising messages, all within Mission Screen. Keep your image reliable regardless of what sort of message you're sending.

For instance, Lyft, a ride-sharing help, exceeds all expectations by giving clients a motivation. Then, at that point, to finish it off, they repeat why their administration is perfect. Riding costs less for clients than an ordinary taxi = cost sharp. Drivers are in every case close by = helpful.

2. *Further develop your client service insight*
To ensure your client support is in excellent condition:
- Be responsive - Ensure you're keeping steady over things. Try not to let clients remarks and questions go unanswered for a really long time. Remain mindful of what's coming in, and what's going out accordingly. However long you show a little adaptability and compassion, clients will be more comprehension when there are issues.
- Be true - The more genuine you are, the better opportunity you need to satisfy a client. The tone you use, and the manner in which you act towards a client, can either represent the deciding moment their experience. In the

event that you're excessively pushy, you might appear to be being tricky. Track down the equilibrium, be deferential, and be useful.
- Be steady - Make repeatable cycles with the goal that all clients are standing out enough to be noticed. Set a few norms for client collaborations. Ensure you have client tagging programming set up that helps make things simpler.

For instance, Zappos has a client care office that exceeds everyone's expectations. One client purchased shoes for her dad, yet he had died before the shoes shown up. The client brought in to check whether she could return the shoes and get discounted. A Zappos call focus worker told her not to stress over sending them back, and that she would be discounted. The worker then, at that point, exceeded all expectations and sent her roses too.

3. *Construct connections, as individuals allude individuals*
Without a doubt, individuals allude individuals and not really the business. That is the reason building associations with your customers is fundamental.

This is particularly significant on the off chance that you're managing clients on a one-on-one premise. You want to ensure you're working really hard of standing by listening to the client and causing them to feel great.

Regardless of whether you work for a huge brand and can't interface with clients one-on-one, you can in any case fabricate connections through your computerized promoting drives. For instance, you can send customized messages that feature a client's singular advantages, advising them that you know them and care about what their identity is. You can likewise share be straightforward. Showing what happens in the background assists clients with seeing who you truly are.

4. *Customize your communications however much you can*
The more you can customize the experience for the client, the more joyful they'll be. Whether that is recollecting data about them, helping them to remember something significant, or sending them a very much planned advancement, personalization shows clients that you give it a second thought.

For instance, on the off chance that a client buys another snowboard from your outdoor supplies site, it's a good idea to convey material that is pertinent to that endorser. You could send data on snow conditions, suggestions for more stuff, or a promotion code for a lift ticket at a neighborhood mountain. On the other hand, on the off chance that somebody buys a b-ball, they could get various suggestions.

Personalization brings about a more drawn in client base, one that is probably going to allude to your companions, family, and partners.

5. Make it a point to inquire

Despite the fact that references frequently happen normally, it very well may be hard to get individuals to ponder you after they leave. That is the reason you ought to continuously request a reference.

As a general rule, clients are normally most joyful post-buy, so this is a great chance to request references. For instance, an internet business store normally requests references their thank you or receipt pages. This cycle can be computerized, making it simple for you.

You can likewise offer motivations to make alluding significantly better. For instance, Booking.com sends an email after a client has made a booking, empowering the client to impart to a companion to get $25 off

6. Show appreciation to those that allude you

Clearly, everybody needs to be valued. Yet, it is especially essential to show appreciation to the people who send more clients your way. On the off chance that somebody alludes you, in addition to the fact that they are offering you a commendation, yet they are making a special effort to help you.

Assuming you can figure out who alluded you, make certain to say thanks to them. You don't be guaranteed to need to do some large or excellent motion, however it is vital to recognize their work. Besides, it will additionally emphasize why they helped you in any case.

Building these sort of profound associations will keep you associated with your objective market. This keeps references coming in.

7. *Begin or further develop your proper reference program*
Having a reference program makes it simple for individuals to make references. Fortunately, there are numerous arrangements out there that can help you track and deal with your program. These arrangements can likewise help you in disseminating rewards.

Regardless of whether you decide to boost your program, formalizing it will guarantee that you're exploiting verbal exchange advertising as you would be able.

For instance, Dropbox began a reference program and offered additional extra room as their motivation. They took an item that individuals need and need and expanded clients rapidly by offering them some additional room, for the two players (the referrer and reference). Since clients had a lot to gain by going for it, sharing followed. After their program was carried out they saw an immense leap in participation recruits with an increment of around 60%.

Regardless of where you are in building your image, references ought to be a fundamental piece of your promoting program. Eventually, suggestions drive organizations forward. With these tips, you ought to have the option to make a more referable business that delights current clients and keeps new ones coming in.

Conclusion

As we bid farewell to the pages of 'The page power : Success Made Simple,' let us carry with us the profound wisdom that success is not measured by the complexity of our strategies, but by the clarity of our vision and the simplicity of our execution. In a world inundated with noise, we have discovered the transformative power of distillation – condensing our ideas, aspirations, and plans onto a single page, where they shimmer with unmistakable clarity. Armed with this newfound understanding, let us venture forth into the realm of marketing, guided by the beacon of simplicity, fueled by the magic that lies within the confines of a solitary page. May we harness this magic to illuminate our path, to inspire action, and to forge connections that transcend the confines of space and time. For in the end, it is not the volume of words we speak or the complexity of our strategies that define our success, but rather the elegance and simplicity with which we communicate our message to the world. And so, as we turn the final page of this book, let us remember: simplicity is not merely a virtue; it is a superpower, capable of transforming the mundane into the extraordinary, the complicated into the comprehensible, and the dreams of today into the realities of tomorrow. Go forth, dear reader, and let the magic of simplicity guide you on your journey to marketing mastery.

www.ingramcontent.com/pod-product-compliance
Lightning Source LLC
Chambersburg PA
CBHW070414230526
45471CB00006B/2793